CIRCADIA

To Peggy Manton,
Thank you for the
great care you gave
to my mother, Helene
on 1/24 for her sinus
balloon surgery by Dr. Wade.
You were very kind to both
of us! Bless you!

A BOOK OF POETRY

[handwritten signature]

HEIDI L. KLOTZMAN

CONTENTS

Alice in Reality

The shade only covers one-third of her face as she walks distant beaches. Bathing suit scorched off. Smile faded into her waterproof lipstick. She appears oblivious to the sunscreen vicariously living through her pores.

Tears flow unknowingly between the salt of the seas and the spice in her eyes, though she notices neither their departure nor the shrinking of currents within.

Squinting out of her designer sunglasses, she hosts an exchange with the fireball of infallible posture. The sun. It lights up the world, but for whose eyes?

She also wonders why some words don't sound how they're spelled and why capital letters are more revered. She assumes the alphabet is home to prejudice too.

She takes another sip of her watered-down iced tea.

The sip trickles down her chin and spills onto her chest, landing on her faded tattoo. It is the remainder of a fist with the pointer finger missing, the middle finger smudged.

One cannot help but notice her skin. It is dry and flaking— her dermis dulled like a ballpoint pen exhausted from overexertion. If one observes closely, one can tell that it hasn't always been this way. Someday, similar to this one, long ago, she must have glowed with the perspiration of protest, beamed with the bliss of revelation.

She had that look about her, that look of maturity through struggle and enlightenment through pain.

Another writer may have rather seen her in her functioning days of young fancies and flights. I, however, am intrigued by the aftermath. It is clear she has already happened.

Combustive

Our poetic saliva collides in a bubbling seltzer.
Somewhere there's a chemist trying to invent a wave like us.
How do I stir you solid, molten of the earth?
My tears melting lava.
Sign says, "Breathe in air, not in water."
I must have sweltered into quicksand.
Was that the plan? To mesh?
Decide which molecule was dirt and which was flesh.
Inhaling shallow oxygen in depth.
I was your right hand. You were my left.
When palms crumbled. Black to blame. The filtered dusk.
Your screeching odoristic musk.
Trickling sideways across in ultraviolet rays of diabetic heat.
Press enter, I delete you, God. Scripted...lock lip did.
Historically...immorally...cryptic. Us in erasable ink did.
Butter wands, but brought no pixie. Rotated negative 360.
So now, my air's worn in carbon.
My prosecuted rhythm is your stardom?
Ignore my paper's margin—you, God.
Pimp slap Joan upside the head with some self-respect.
Paralyzing limbs to inspect her finale, inside the letter O.
She's seeing circles, but the camera got her swearin'
That she's living the commercial. So bled the beam,
Choking on melodic chorals of her own bloodstream,
Never to redeem the stolen fetish.
All they could smell was chlorine, a saltine dream.
The air coughed; the dust wheezed.
Jesus said, "Oh God,
I forgot to cross my ts. Does it make you proud?"
God: "Oh yes, son.
I believe in all numbers between zero and none."
Instead of trying to condense the latest menace,
Who by the way, isn't Dennis.
So you ask, "Where's the lava, where's my crust?
Am I visually just—red, white and blue folic hair
To accessorize your patriotic flair?
You were my truth; I, your dare.
Passed go, collect 200—didn't find you there.
You, my molten of the earth   evaporated.

Remi

It is golden brown and flat to the touch.
It meets in perpendicular lines
To form squares on each face of its neck.
It is blocked, closed, and often forgotten in the house
Like leftovers are when delivery rings the doorbell.

It does not complement its surroundings.
When you shake it,
You hear only subtle proof of any occupancy at all.
Lends nothing to the memory of a lit, living Aries.
It is hard to believe that a dog rests inside its domain,
Her early flesh snuffed out of existence.

Whether it is rocked on its head, side or bottom,
It remains nothing more than a wooden box,
Sealed for the duration,
A period susceptible to being hastened.
Yet it still sits on your shelf as a token of remembrance,
The acceptable memento of paid respect to a loyal pet.

I still wonder who could receive comfort from it.
It lacks her soggy kiss,
Her rambunctious limbs and her late night hymns,
Distinct to her—now ever melodious.

Secretly, I cannot help but be curious
Of the scent and sight of ash, beloved ash.
Has corruption peaked in me
That I would be so bold as to unseal her fate?
Remi, Remi, I beg that you are far,
Far from this quadrilateral cell.
I wish that we'd not have this relation.

Even in my most cynical mood,
I caress this dulled manifestation of you,
Groping to find something familiar.

The Color of His Eyes

Blast their holy efforts.
One could never baptize God enough
To reach your blue.
Ice hot steam piercing my whole.
My synergy branded
As if heaven's cloud is blue aflame.
Blue singes go my pores, blue silence go my veins.
Blue chill in hot blood.
My fever, your flame; your love, my stain.
Hypnotic—tropical breeze, be still.
But how can I smear?
I stick your wind in my lung,
But word embarrasses you.
You are more. My faucet, my food.
The source of my hunger and thirst.
Oh, he blinks.
Engulf me in ocean blue sound; I am ears.
Though to you, I remain
Just a cloud in a ribbon of sky.
Just a stray pearl in an ocean of oyster.
Just a mermaid on dry plains
With no limbs to walk to you. No use to you now.
Dry itching freedom, blue sky.
Can you rain; can you blacken?
I drown, lose being in your eyes.
I am of you.
You have not yet been informed. Know now.
I am depth; I am deep.
For your waking, I am sleep.
Pools rise here in whirls.
Ocean stand; I am bounty in my hope
That here in my darker, brown eyes,
You'll breathe ocean—breathe fire—you'll love me.
Be in me. Touch my sand; hold my steam.
When color fades two into one.
Inside blue sky, meet brown sun.

Immunity to Antibiotics

The symmetry of our eye
Cons my devon forever wind.
Call those wild.
Came by forest, went by sea.
Pipeline, glory peppered rhapsody.
Not a note you sing.
Speak through me.
It's not just another love, but falls where I catch me.

Shall I comb through disheveled threads of mystery
Or adhere to my native history
Of membrane depleted, heart de-meated,
Periodic table defiance?
'Cause we got chemistry, but it ain't about science.
Appetites hungry for lozenges.
Cough syrup community.

We got shot by the doctor, be it needle or gun.
Said we'd be protected from the common flu,
But not hate or fear, or more contagious—love.

In the beauty of poems and art,
Immersed in the blueprint of colors and scriptures
Which decorate our toxins
Of fiberglass tiles and hearts,
We shall not forget the agony,
The underlying pain that went unsoothed,
Thus fueling this explosion of reality.
Intercept it.

"None Left to Speak for Me"
From a sign at The Holocaust Museum

We discredit our rage poets
Because we think they complain more than they solve.
We discredit our bliss poets
Because we think they omit the world's thirst.
We discredit our neutral poets
Because we think they don't side with conviction.

We discredit all our poets
Because their imagery is seldom apparent;
Their sentiment, hardly sound;
Their vision, rarely concrete.

We discredit all rage, all bliss, all neutrality.
We discredit oral history and future possibility
When we discredit all our poets.

For the Boy Who Surprises Me

He reaches out.
He listens.
He comforts.
He advises.
He hears her tear herself apart
And tells her she is beautiful once more.

He understands her.
No one does.
He validates her cries,
Wiping away her tears without even knowing,
Kissing away her scars, all inflamed and raised.

Truth runs through his words like the river wild,
Rupturing the walls of her overflowing dam.
No fabrications.
No cheap thrills.
He's the realest kind of real.
Her evergreen transcending season.

He believes.
He makes her believe.
She heals
With his genuine helping heart
Beating firm inside her chest.

He lives
Daringly and vividly all around her,
Challenging her to shine alongside him.
He loves.
She returns his love.
He may think he is all alone.
He is not.
She is…   I am here with

                    You.

More Than

Many write music. Many play music.
Many have rhythm. Many even sway to that rhythm.

But very few give birth to, give death to,
Surrender to its avenue beyond walking distance.
Even fewer choose to see beyond their rose-colored vision,
As if the rose's thorns had pricked them,
They would've bled a rainbow of sound.

Those few would neither display nor frame the holy rays
By calling them profit or success.
Instead, they would insert them into veins,
And call them by their names of either sun, daughter, or joy.
A collage of sweat-ridden beat, grit,
And undefined fields they'd cultivate
By the instinct of mother's milk and heart meat.
Even past tremors would do them justice
By resurfacing as newfound depth, maturity, resilience.

Their burdens would stare into the reflection
Of their sun, daughter, or joy
And balance their wavering tension,
Knead their muscled knot of doubt
Into a driven, flammable acid.
Drinkable only by lovers who fight, fighters who love
And thus have spiritual intercourse with their internal enemy.
In the setting of the eternal now.
Where all that has mattered is gone,
And all that is gone has mattered.

They still kneel and cleanse to become a part of the music
Without asking for a contract,
Permanence, or the promise of immortality.
They'd rather be marked, stained, swallowed,
Drained into the music.

Those few are more than subtle accessories to sound.
I know one of those few.
He who does not only play an instrument, he who is one.

Mas Que

Muchos escriben musica. Muchos aun tocan musica.
Muchos tienen ritmo. Muchos aun bailan a ese ritmo.

Pero pocos dan luz a, dan la muerte a, se ceden a la calle
Mas alla que la distancia que caminar.
Pocos ven fuera de su vision rosada.
Como si cuando las espinas de las rosas.
Les habia picado sangraron un arco iris.
Una cinta de sonido.

Entonces, esos pocos no mostrarian ni encerrarian
Esas rayas sagradas.
Ni siguiera las llamarian por provecho o exito.
Se las inyectarian en los venos.
Y las llamarian por sus nombres los de sol, hija, o felicidad.
Un colaje de ritmo, cascajo sudados,
Y campos sin nombre cultivarian
Por instinto animal, por leche maternal, carne de Corazon.
Aun terremotos les justificarian reaparecion de hondo
Nuevo, madurez, y resalto.

Su carga fijaria la refleccion de su sol, hija, o felicidad.
Y balancearia su tension disigual.
Amasaria su nudo musculoso de duda
En un acido ardiente y arojando.
Solamente potable por enamorados que se guerran,
Guerrerros que se enamoran.
Y asi llegan a una copola espiritual con su enemigo interno.
En el fondo del ahora eterno.
Donde todo lo que importo se fue
Y todo lo que se fue importa ya.

Arrodillandose y purificando, tratando de pertenecer,
compartir la musica sin pedir un contrato, permenencia,
Ni la promesa de inmortalidad.
Preferirian estar marcado, manchado, tragado,
Chupado hasta la musica.

Esos pocos son mas que accesorios sutiles al sonido.
Conozco a esos pocos que
No solamente toca instrumento musicale. El es uno.

Idealistic Rut?

I'd rather feel deeply than think practically.
Rather die as a nut than live as a rock,
Watching the leaves rustle,
Envying the bark's honeysuckle sap.
Rather lay on the outcast lap of forbidden fruit
Than on the sanctioned cloud, as dense as it is thin.
Fools may rush in where angels fear to tread,
But fools, they lack the fear that angels harbor.

His Potential

When you break bread with word crumbs
And spread poetry for jam,
You both numb and heighten every sense.
Paralyzing and igniting my emotional spine.
Fear not, my pride. Birthing my heart to race.
There's a will to beat again.
Once a corpse asleep from the world, you awaken me.

Electrifying a coma of a sky.
Not with the lightning rod, but with the source.
Not the vowels or consonants you speak,
But by the heart that's breaking underneath.
By your masked face that you only think I can't see.
By your glow beneath the shade.
You only think you don't shine.

Keys, being poems, unlock you, revealing a truer reflection.
The bruise that never did heal. The smile that never did fade.
Once a poem, now a mirror.
Makes you wonder what exactly you were seeing
Before you had sight.

I can't see you in burning coal blackness.
I can't hear you in muted sound.
I can't touch you on the other side of the mirror.
But I don't have to see or hear or touch to feel
Every passion that flames in a heart you swear is hollow.
You've tried. The poem may escape you,
But you won't escape the poem.

I've tried. But when it spills off the tresses of your lips, I melt.
Blood replaced by sweet, stinging syrup.
Panting in my sweat, I refuse hydration.
Lost in a dimension of visible sounds, of decibel colors,
With light as reflection and volume as number.
Found in a love yet undefined.

Why is it making me cry? It's just a poem.
Why is it making me love you? You're just a friend.

The Poem My English Teacher Walked Out On

If a meteor crashing is just a sign of Earth,
The explosion that I feel inside is just a sign of birth.
Mother natured me a splinter of Hollywood sin,
For the only heart worth breaking
Is the heart I'm beating in.
Circumference in circles
To all the places my heart has gone—
My head has never been.
Your sugar, my cavity. Novocain, five-second friend.
Deception rules my traveling shoes
With a carnival for truth.
Where all the rides are free,
Sure, if you work at every booth.
A one-way street; I get hit, traced by authorities in vain.
He may wear a badge, but the motive's all the same.
All of the sudden, traffic goes spastic,
Eradicated by the ultraviolet spark.
Despite my darkness, mark this down as another sin.
Denial hidden in the excess of the gin.
No more tiger to tame.
My echo heard in a planet undiscovered,
An expletive they call my name.
And expect me to answer?
The world is bacteria;
Still you blame me for my cancer?
Alas, we're on the same level as you talk, and I listen.
No matter silk nor grain,
Not all blue eyes have the glisten.
But tears spilling out of these eyes could mean I'm
Happy enough to cry?
Be my guide as you walk beside me,
Not behind me in the trenches.
Ironic that life's best players are busy—
Taking up space along the benches.
The clenches, my fists aren't bringing me to strike.
My identity shattered—might as well just be like Mike.

Was that your ammunition that fueled the third Reich?
Are my words hot enough to spark a forest fire?
Between her limbs is all you desire.
I'll live and rest in peace
Even if mercy is just a handicap in your eyes.
Such as a boy having feelings, God forbid, tears.
Me living in his name; is that your only fear?
In a perception that censors my breathing air.
Your voice in my throat—how did that get there?
But on paper is not the vapor I give off into the air.
Your skepticism, your every prison, is not just bars;
There's a ceiling there.
I know you say that's worse; a ceiling means an end.
A first page means a last one.
A man who's straight will eventually bend.
But why lie; I'm in love.
Give me a good enough reason, and I'll pretend,
But look you in the eye,
And say I don't see more than just a friend?
The grapevine is just scribbling ink in vain into the air.
So what if your body shows up if your heart isn't there?
When one is indecisive, one must choose.
If one team wins the game, the other one must lose.
Are you that determined
To walk your life in someone else's shoes?
All your green doesn't compensate
For what you haven't learned.
Another dollar spent is a dollar less earned.
The nature-loving say,
If there's a rock, leave it unturned.
But if it's hell you wish for,
Then it's hell for which I'll burn.
The professor has spoken her final word.
Today, you are my student.
Tomorrow, I may have never occurred.

Haikus

People once told me
That I was somehow too deep,
And then they all drowned.

In America,
Only a foreign accent
Can be familiar.

Children are not told
That their beloved playgrounds
Will be parking lots.

Deep hearts are roomy
And can easily recover.
Shallow hearts are doomed.

Live quietly if
You're living for approval.
Live loud for true love.

Teammates huddle tight.
Sweat entwines, and one athlete
Leaves the structure dry.

Alarm wakes children.
Minus eggs, they leave for school
With combat boots on.

Together alone.
Every time that we hold hands,
I count five fingers.

Unattainable Emcees

You harmonized tonight.
And with every song you sang,
A little piece of me laid itself down on the floor,
And said, "Take me, too."

And you sang the song off the song sheet.
And you took the part of me off the floor,
Teaching me to internalize the score.

Encompassing the range I wanted to reach.
With you inspiring me to believe.
That a numb girl can feel.
That a mute girl can sing.
And somehow, life is worth the song.

Food for Thought Poisoning

Kid.
Kid in candy store.
Wide-eyed wonder.
Glory, gum bubbles.
Dreamy, laughing sparkles.

Candy world. Candy land.
Kid. Candy. Candy store.

Feels real. Feels true.
Smells sweet. Tastes good.
Thinks wow, now, love—
Piece of chocolate peace.

Kid grew up.
No longer kid in candy store.
Kid is Bill.
Bill in bank.
Check-bouncing Bill.

Bill walks by candy store.
Loses his appetite.
Bad taste in his mouth.

Bad taste for kid.
For candy.
For store.
For childhood.
For growing.
For dying.
For life.

In candy store.
In money store.
Outside of either.
Inside of both.

Hypothetical

If birth and death spring from the same mother,
How come we run from one and towards the other?

Zero years old. My almost birthday.
God saw I was lonely,
Even lonelier than him in vacuous heaven.
So he gave me a toy for company
While I waited to be born.

I still remember it.
It was a female, action figure with large, breast plates
Holding a sword in her left hand, a nail file in her right.
(Some She-Ra meets Skipper giveaway.)
Publicity stunt or not, God was PC that day.

Anyway, I figured that for her to be a true action figure,
She'd have to figure out some action.
So I hopped on her oily back,
Absorbed the emanation of her pores
And rode her all the way to church.
Unlike heaven, church was populated.

I felt like the meat inspector at a vegetarian café—
Completely irrelevant.
And still, I remember overdosing on prunes
Hoping to induce a poetic vowel movement in you,
God, who turned out to be absent at the time.

Before I am born,
I might as well join my action figure counterpart
Who's estranged from both
The rise and fall of mind and heart.

If birth and death spring from the same mother,
Why do we run from one and towards the other?

Got Scope?

He'll never remember how I looked at sunrise
With morning breath and crusted lashes.

He can't think fondly of my effortless glow,
My holding back, my subtle hum.

I never showed him understated.
I gave it all.

I dressed the role and did cartwheels in circles.
I walked the tight rope and made the seven seas part.

But it's a play, and I was starring,
While he was searching
                              for an extra.

Nature Teaches

As the dead flowers of last year

Rise again and begin to bloom,

I watch in awe.

Even I could be different.

Feminista: Taking Herself Back

Like she says to Jason—"Be patient. I'm doctor."
As she prescribes the internal percussion,
Leaving silence open for discussion.
Mute to every word that her hips don't utter.
Should've called her by her species and not her race.
A color is just a void in which to fill a space.
Sometimes she separates within her skin.
Compromised often, like the color of her eyes,
Fading and darkening to suit your every mood.
If only she could wear a brain and still be in the nude.
You as transparent, she sees through
Your dictionary, vague definition
Of her in any compromised position.
Whatever angle happens to fit
The moral of your unmusical instrument.
Excuse her truth—she means emotional impotence.
Just leave your mooning to the night,
Your quenching to the Sprite.
Your nature is you fight and then flight.
But even without fists to fight, wings to fly,
She whiffs you, a withering petal,
Thinking your approval more Olympic than the medal.
Platinum, in fact, is your vocab as your opinion swells,
Imprinting heaven as two, twin hells,
Profiting off her blood.
Sure, it must taste sweet
As you capture her inside your beat.
Got bulletproof amplifiers to keep you from
Sucking on her like your inhaler for hire—
You don't even have asthma.
If the cradle rocked the world,
Who rocked the universe? Your cytoplasm?
Does your memory extend her
As further than a spell or curse?
A hefty substance arousing both hunger and thirst?

So you can eat and drink her 'til she's gone?
'Til she's a nation sans population?
Do what your words mean or what you mean
By your words incite the assassination?
Your wicked wit leads her to her finale, a timely exit.
How many seconds before the next chick?
Never feared her heart
Would need a love proof vesting.
Not from bullets of fire.
Flame is too icy a word to label on mere desire.
For the devil's bed she's burning in.
Call the Congress' whole damn clergy in.
As the verdict surfaces from beneath the skin.
A scab, her recovery.
And still for her earnings, you're lusting?
How many notches to your right
Does she mind adjusting?
Ask her again when the pus breaks the skin open.
Breaking is more popular than being broken.
Beat dead heart; the moon is not the only star.
But being the typical dame,
She refrains in fear of bruising her open scar.
Well, at least shade her lines in between.
The damned ocean on her face
Is not her natural sheen.
Is it really the thought that matters
Behind the 10 dollar versus 10 million gift?
Here recipient—wrap this future.
You think both hearts will benefit?
Are you prepared to stare the question in its answer
If it means that knowing why
Is the extinction to the stanza?

Brainchild

I'm trembling because I wrote something beautiful
That I can call mine and love as my child.
And I don't have to worry about keeping it alive
Because as long as hearts beat, it will live.

And when I am long gone and dead of many years,
Some girl will read her own poetry
And cry her own tears.
She will finally be content in knowing
That she doesn't need a man or friend
Or relative or career to love her
In order for her to love herself.
That is a woman's destiny.

Airport Mentality

I feel most free in airports.
Suspended in time.
Nowhere.
Not from, not to.
Just waiting in the middle.
Blissfully non-pressured.
Breathing in and out.
Peeling through pages of magazines.
Having a sandwich.
Smiling at passersby.
This is not a time to worry.
It is a time to be idle.
I enjoy it like a cradle.
Like a child again, returning home.

Capacity Minus Opportunity

This is how a disconnected wire must feel.
So capable
Of sparking a guiding light,
But instead remaining unplugged for the duration.
Failing to establish any lasting relation.

Human beings, little ink spots upon the page.
In solitude, they connect themselves,
The dots that are the game.
All connected, they imply as if to unify.
Disconnected they remain.

Filled up on Empty

I don't know whether it's a character strength or defect
That I can't turn emotions off once on.
Without compassion, who is of much use,
But without self-restraint,
Who can survive these fickle moods?

Following one's heart is a hazard
Without guidance from one's mind.
We're like infants frozen by the awe of snow,
Children tempted by sugars
And salts and salves for tastes that go.

To temper these cravings is to deny,
But to obey all impulse is to recklessly comply.
Lips that were once smooth are now sharpened.
If you can be cut by a kiss,
What damage could a weapon inflict?

In content, we are confused atoms.
In style, we seem assured adults.
Honesty is preached, but not rewarded.
Results often come to those who hold back.

We attempt to empty out our heavy hearts
To feel lighter, to visibly shine.
We know that they know
Our clutter isn't far behind our daily grind.

You can't trust you
When your type is not consistent with your welfare.
You look into mirrors and men's eyes
And are ashamed of what you see in there.
Straddling two equally threatening fears;
One of being too close, one of being too alone.

I envy those who invest
Only after they're certain it's returned.
While I contemplate wisdom, they implement it.
I study you and wonder what I've learned.

Snow Grows Outside of Brooklyn

Snowballs. Snow cones. Falling snow.
Celebrate the mood.

Snowmen. Snow fairies. Snow sculptures.
Children play around it.

Snowflakes. Snowed in. Snow-capped mountains.
What a breathtaking view.

Snow sniffed. Snow thrown. Snow blown.
Now it's inside of you.

Cocaine. Heroin.
It's candy, escaping, and fuel.
It's trendy, happening,
And craving your system immune.

If you turn to snow,
You face down with the light of the mirror,
And melt with the heat of the sun.

Today they've predicted a snowstorm for fun,
But the trouble is not just the storm.
It's what my friends have become.

Spoiled Rotten

We women really have no grounds to reprimand.
We perpetuate the cycle
That gives you men the upper hand.
It's not your fault that you think you can get over.
We teach you that it works; we enable you to own us.
This also means that since we put you where you are,
We can deliver you back.
But how many women are attempting to do that?
We build your throne, solidify your place,
And sign off on the arrogance across your face.
We bat our lashes, refill our glasses,
And flatter your smallest acts of kindness.
While we compete for your approval,
Our thoughts reflect the facts,
And our emotions lead us to be foolish.
As we wait, analyze, strategize, and squirm,
You are amused by treating us to your very own terms.
You were once a humble spirit—
Curious, open, and warm.
We muddled your role and ruined your form.
We spoiled you rotten.
Yet we are surprised every single time,
We sink our teeth in
To find you have gone stale.

Self-absorption:
The Bell Jar's Inner View

I traveled
Far, far away in my head.
The natives of lands would laugh at me
Because they had never seen
What I'd seen in their homes.
They'd never known the newness and ripe glows.
They had lost their awe the longer they had lived,
Especially for home.

I'd stare at their leaf-like formations
For uncountable hours.
I'd sit in the middle of busy roads
To catch oncoming traffic.
It felt as if a foundation had risen below my two feet
The more I got lost in my head.

These trips weren't daydreams.
It wasn't day.
It wasn't dreaming.
I was experiencing intuitive scopes
And remnants of memories dissolve and rename.

Tempted seldom by the outside world to escape,
I swore off all danger and played it safe.
My head.
My only place to vacate.

Safe

If I never knew love,
I wouldn't know what I was missing.
If the party hadn't started,
I wouldn't feel the void upon its ending.

I want someone to go home to
After all the schmoozing's through.
I just want to cuddle
And be held 'til warmth becomes the truth.
I want to be safe in a place that will not harm me.
I want to be safe in your arms.

If you weren't unavailable,
Then I would not still be searching.
If you came too easy,
My soul would not have known the yearning.

I want my privacy, my independence,
My freedom, and your acceptance.
I want to be moved,
But done so gently.
I want you, but only if you want me
To be safe in your arms.

Playing with Letters

A love sought a B for effort.
C he was no D-lister.
Evolved and wickedly handsome.
F that. G was like scoring H
After texting only one number in your phone.
I warned her that Jaywalking
Across the tracks to exit K
Was a bit dangerous with the L train coming and all,
But she was determined that
We had to have that kind of night.
We were on eMpty, but spilling oil,
Nearing ENron's favorite pastime.
She continued to fill up on Opiates she found,
Never minding other people's P's and Q's.
After they took hold, she started confessing to me
That her weaknesses R ESTee Lauder,
UV Rays from a bed, beach, or bottle, and don't
W know, each and every eX-boyfriend.
Y? Because from A-Z,
None of them are too easy to find.
Don't you know that's when I got out of there.

Villanelle to the Contrary

They say that there is nothing new under the sun,
that all imagery has been reduced to dead metaphor.
There must be an art yet to have been seen or made or
done.

There are definitely voices yet to grace the air waves,
faces that instead prefer to leave methods of exaltation
to the gods. They say that there is nothing new under
the sun.

Writers, by their feathers, feud over whether there is
still such a thing as inspiration remaining among a
nation of willing franchise, where few do tell the primary
from the plagiarized. Still, there must be an art yet to
have been seen or made or done.

I wish to tell those writers, this inspiration does not walk
about wearing a sign. Like most things worthy of
noting, you will not hear of them; we will not hear of
them; they will not hear of themselves. They say that
there is nothing new under the sun.

Is our world not a melting pot boiling over modest
talent, an unaware cesspool of uncrowned jewel?
There must be an art yet to have been seen or made
and done.

Along with the jewel, the underdog is he who barks well
in his sleep. It takes an attentive mother, a listening
poet, to hear those silent barks and spot those hidden
jewels. They say that there is nothing new under the
sun. There must be an art yet to have been seen or
made or done.

To the Self-righteous

You may know where God lives.

That doesn't mean you're invited.

A Long Way Ahead. A Long Way Behind.

I know I'm not over you
Because I want to know where you are right now,
And I've already found out.

I know I'm not over you
Because you buzz through my thoughts and feelings
Like a nagging season fly.

I know I'm not over you
Because no journal has enough pages,
No pen enough ink,
No textbook enough words to explain my longing.

I know I'm not over you
Because I fantasize of how you will apologize
Even though it is I who you say is to blame.

I know I'm not over you
Because I can't raise enough interest out of me
To open my heart to deserving suitors in my path.

I know I'm not over you
Because the imagery of your tantalizing eyes,
Broad shoulders, distinctive walk, freckled back,
Soothing tone, air of mystery, boyish whining,
Wavy hair, guitar-ready hands, bitten nails,
And unmistakable voice
Still beckons me beyond logic, sanity, reason,
And all of the guidance I've received.

I know I'm not over you
Because I still crave your calls,
Messages, and presence,
As toxic and damaging as it is and you are.

I know I'm not over you
Because of the guilty pang in my gut,
Pondering whether I really did betray you
By not helping you enough
Or in the right way or anything enough.

I know I'm not over you
Because I want to roll back the slides
And take back every moment
Where I spilled my soul
Like warm milk into your empty glass.
I should have held back.

I know I'm not over you
Because instead of writing about flowers
Or summer or news,
I am caught rambling,
Scribbling down all I can remember of you.

I know I'm not over you
Because my hand is tired, and yet,
I will keep on spinning,
Circling about my conquest, not yet conquered,
In clear sight of the fact that the arrow routes a U-turn,
Finding its way without fail
To the center of my open heart.

Comfort Zone Blown

We have to leave to come back.
We have to flee to know home.
We have to. We must.
Just as we have to be born to die,
We have to die to be reborn.
We have to. We must.
We have to fall to bounce above.
We have to fail at life and love.
We have to give thanks for inconveniences of growth.

Mortal Meets Immortal

Why bother to write?
We could be living our images.
Sometimes it's hard to tell
Whether writing is making us crazy or keeping us sane.

It's not a stable art.
Neither a shoulder to cry on
Nor an unconditional friend.
'Cause that writer's block is a poet's broken heart,
And no between-the-sheet sequence with man
Can replace the release of the right words expressed.

Often it's the words themselves that fail to be recalled.
It's the message we retain.
The togetherness we crave.
Communication overdue.
The humbling realization that our poems will outlive us.
So, why bother to write?

To foresee how we are remembered.

Depressive Episodes

So possessed, a peril gray.
Road kill among the mind.
Clear the road so we may travel.
Rid the waste so we may lead.
Oh, a perfect peace in solitary nothing.
No fall, no climb.
No need to reach or be.

A Hopeful Romantic

I want someone to share epiphanies with at 3:38 a.m.
Who hears Ndegeocello moaning,
"Tell me I'm the only one," and really feels it.
I want someone who doesn't end.
Someone who turns the bold color yellow
In this gothic state, unafraid to be blinding.
I want someone who appreciates the wisdom in
Children, jazz, the elderly, silence, and history.
I want someone who does as much as I dream.
Someone who spells ancient hieroglyphics
With their tongue.
I want someone who can describe the sky,
And replace all temptation to get high.
I want someone who can withstand
My many moods and masks and fables.
Someone who feels humbled by all that is.
I want someone who reads between my wrinkles.
Someone who swears by traveling to build perspective.
I want someone who makes me never want to sleep
Again for fear of missing a moment of them.
Someone who revels in the process,
The country drive as a detour,
And enjoys when the electricity goes out.
Someone who cherishes their memories as much.
I want someone who gets goose bumps when
MLK speaks and feels rage when a swastika appears.
Someone to experience the 60s with.
I want someone to be in awe of me—sometimes.
Someone who has the curiosity to want to try a drug
And the willpower to refuse to.
Someone who makes me, not fall, but rise into love.
Someone who I feel no awkwardness with when bare.
I want someone who says,
"Don't deprive the world of your talent,"
And isn't pretending.
Someone who teases my frame

And then devours it like a juicy tenderloin.
I want someone whose words have mobile limbs.
Someone who is a modest and timely poet.
I want someone who can keep themselves busy
While I'm strumming guitar or blankly zoning.
Someone who needs no reason to hug,
To call, to encourage, to give.
I want equality and chivalry.
I want sacred love and naughty lust.
I want God and answers.
Someone with a tranquil pool in their eyes
For me to lose time in.
I want someone without agenda, but with suggestions.
I want the fairytale, the office with a view,
And my money back.
I want someone who really digs quotes.
Someone whole who I don't have to tailor.
I want someone
Who has a pregnant woman's cravings with me.
I want a pet without scent,
Freedom without responsibility.
Wait—is this about the someone I want or me?

Meant to Be

Some things that are meant to be
Just don't happen.

Many things that are thought are not said.
Many things that are dreamt go unrealized.

What we could be is only potential energy.
It becomes kinetic when it drops;
Real only once it hits the ground.

Some things that are meant to be just don't happen.
Some love that is supposed to evolve is blocked.

When fear overshadows possibility,
A blank canvas stays blank.
A glowing star shines alone in a dark, basement room.
And we never quite become "us."

They say that if it is meant to be, it will be.
But if we stand in the way of what is meant,
How do we know if what is not happening
Wasn't actually in order to take place,
Had we not buried the feeling,
Sworn off the idea,
And snuck away at the first sign of light?

Tentative Vows

I cannot escape.
Both my daydreams and night dreams
Inform me of you.

I crave you more than water or food.

I am enticed.
I have rang twice,
And your voice message is the last sound I hear
Before I drift into slumber.

I want to be eavesdropping the day
You first tell your mother,
"I love her."

I want to have your children and be your wife.
I want to be the only woman in your life.
I want to help you accomplish your goals
And stand beside you when everyone else
Realizes the brilliance in you that I've always known.

Equity

Everyone's changing and growing
While I'm scared to step out of line.
I used to draw outside the box,
But now it's the only place I can hide.

Everyone's marrying and babying and careering
While I'm scared to meet life today.
It's not the language I'm used to hearing.
I'm afraid of what it might say.

Where did the time go?
All that chasing and hiding.
Primping for the next best distraction.

I should know this song in full on guitar by now.
I should be playing it for my children soon.
But before I have them, must have a partner.
And before a partner, a date.
Before that, a solid career and financial stability.
The preface to everything—my prelude to the world.
The wall between the life I live and the one I want.

In the shadow of the shadow, I loom.
And my pain is a beast riding on the coattails
Of every dreaded negotiation.

Start the night with a glass of wine or three to become free.
Waking with the regrets of the shot or two
That slipped through.
The handsome metaphor sleeping next to you.

The cells in my body are bursting
From some sort of emotional carbonation.
I'm fizzing inside like a shaken soda with a stubborn lid.

You get comfortable, even in the meantime.
Even in frustration, you start to cope. Aiming only to keep up.
Running backwards, racing to stand still.
A mouse on the wheel.

Inspired by Bésame Mucho

Don't tell me lies to ease my mind.
I know who you are.
But knowing never stopped me before.

From following the pathway of desire to your side.
My heart spilling contents
On your sheets that leave no stain.
Unscathed you were then, and still you remain.

I am involved, but not blind.
Aware of the spin—your conquer, my divide.
Do not know for how long, but for now, I'm entwined.

Now please tell me those lies to ease my mind.
I can't move your heart, but you change my mind.

Say you are faithful
With your heart, mind, body, and eyes.
That the more I show I feel
Won't scare you off like most mankind.
I want to believe only what keeps this current alive.

I've seen that all waves break onto shore without fail.
I stand by and watch,
Wishing no shore would rise to prevail.

I'd suspend the waves in flowing motion
So that there is no time.
Just a repeating hello without its inevitable goodbye.

I still imagine what makes me happy
Making you happy too.
But who has ever fought nature and won?
As I gain distance for a more objective view,
It is clear that what's deeply changed me
Has barely touched you.

Inspirado por Bésame Mucho

No me diga mentiras para facilitar mi mente.
Sé quién eres. Pero sabiendo nunca me paro' antes.

De seguir el camino del deseo a tu lado.
Mi corazón que derrama el contenido en tus hojas,
Esa licencia ninguna mancha.
Indiferente entonces estabas, y todavía tu permanece.

Estoy implicado, pero no oculto.
Enterado de la vuelta tu conquiste, mi se dividen.
No sepa para cuánto tiempo,
Pero para ahora, estoy entralazada.

Ahora por favor dígame esas mentiras
Para facilitar mi mente.
No puedo mover tu corazón, pero cambias mi mente.
Opinión eres fiel con su corazón,
Mente, cuerpo, y ojos.
Que cuanto más me demuestro siéntome,
Tu no asustaras fácilmente
Como la mayoría de la humanidad.

Deseo creer
Solamente qué mantiene esta corriente viva.
He visto que todas las ondas
Se rompen sobre orilla sin falta.
Hago una pausa y el reloj, no deseando ninguna orilla
Se levantaría para prevalecer.

Suspendería las ondas en el movimiento que fluye
De modo que no haya hora.
Apenas un hola de repetición sin su inevitable adiós.
Todavía me imagino qué me hace feliz
Haciéndoles feliz también.
¿Pero quién ha luchado la naturaleza
Y ha ganado siempre? Como gano distancia para una
Visión más objetiva, la está claro que qué
Profundamente se cambia me le has tocado apenas.

Existential Break

My persona and I are strangers.
Each walks a lonely path.
My spirit is muffled,
Afraid of losing one side to the other.

My persona and I are strangers.
We fight every night.
Persona wants status, press,
Adoration, glamour, and well—everyone.

"I" want peace, family, friendship, justice,
Nature, love, community,
Creative expression through my dreams,
A best friend, soul mate,
And the mastery of simple pleasures.

My persona talks often.
I am spiritual, sensual,
Political, sensitive, and daydreaming
That I somehow save my mother
From any harsh reality.

My persona surrounds me with a guest list of fans
And then leaves me needy and lonely
With outstretched hands.

My persona and I are strangers,
But its bed is my bed,
And its number, my number.
And this poem, our outcry.

Espanola Way

Lust comes over me.
It's like a sunburn within.
There is no reason for it,
And every reason to resist,
But the go-getter persists.

There's nothing like a crush.
New and not knowing.
The novelty of the first night,
A fever in the wind that's blowing.

The flavor and the lighting.
The wishing and the waiting.
The wondering and second-guessing.
The compulsion and impressing.

So controlled in one affair.
Adrift in this other.
Spinning—my stomach swirling.
I think I've missed this feeling.

It's never lead me to contentment—only astray.
But every time I smell the scent of challenge,
It charms my breath away.

Sabotage

Filled with tears that will rot into tomorrow's rain,
I wash my hair and nails and floors
In with all the stains.
The discovery is morbid yet again.
Act different, and so will they,
Mama said.

But what Mama didn't say was, screw them.
What Mama didn't say was, don't take it.
What Mama didn't show
In her example as she froze was that
Papa wasn't good enough for her.

In fact, Mama never told me
That I'd look at each man in front of me
And feel the abandonment of Papa
When he left the room,
When he didn't call,
Or when a pause was too long.
Mama, I can only blame you for so long.

This last one gave me hope, Mama.
I'm scared of what you went through.
I so much want to love, Mama.
Can you see the conflict that ensues?
I see myself identify
And take upon your role sometimes,
And nothing ever satisfies. No one.

You finally left him. Took you so long.
But you did, and I'm proud, Mama.
You showed me a woman's strength.
You finally said "I'm Done," and went your way.
Now help me, Mama.
Help me leave every time
With the same dignity that you stayed.

Relapse

Sometimes my heart stops beating.
Sometimes I enjoy the pain.
Sometimes the colors in the darkness
Mark my way in vain.
Sometimes I can't say no to no.
I just ignore the sun.
The night has shades that spell my name.
And when I wake to you, I know I've won.

I Want it All

I want it all.

Everything and nothing less.
The rhythm of success.
The aftershock of your caress.
The goals accomplished in duress.
That place you took me in my mind.
The beat beneath the rhyme.

I want it all.

Emotions curdle, and they blend.
I feel it, and press send.
There's so much bound inside.
Rings of pleasure. Miles of cries.

I want it all.

Commitment to this moment.
Terrified of never knowing.
The space between is growing.
The distance triples time.
I thought you put what I had put upon the line.

Tell me I can't ruin it.
That you won't let me self-destruct.
Pick me up. Let me fall.
Meet me there. And never budge.

I said I want it all.
And I meant it all with you.

The Side of Me

Today I was born again,
Reborn as myself.
The fears that used to guide
My thoughts and ways
Are distant memories in decay.

I feel at home in my skin and open to adventure.
I want to see other cultures.
Feel my empathy pool into a curdle of warmth.
Over and over, get the point.

The box I lived in was
One of many.
I thought it was the world.
The bubble I danced in,
One of millions
In a carbonated glass.
I killed myself to make it last.

Like the earth
Who looks at other planets
As if she were
An only child.

Travel, God, and family
Brought me here.
I'm happy and accept the way things are.
There's nothing better
That could be.
There's nothing different
That should be.
I'm finally on the side of me.

Swim, Fish

Any size or quality of fish can look big in a bathtub.
Do you have what it takes
To survive in a larger domain?

It just means making a real impact where you are.
It means doing what only you can do.
It means having a spark
That no one can learn or practice.

It means that the light you have in you may burn out
What you thought were real friendships.
It means that you may give everything
You have to someone
Only for them to take it and run
When you need them most.
It means that life is all tangled up,
And we aren't armed with all the info
To make sense of it.

Aim for something vast,
Creative, and spiritually rewarding
That has nothing to do with a career.
When you achieve oneness with your outlets,
You radiate love.

That love will attract people who understand you.
That love will endure the world's rejections.
That love will overpower the weaknesses
That hope to possess your mind and time.

Swim, fish,
In that body of water that frightens you most.
You will return to who you are.

Today

This poem is from today.
There will only be one today.
There will also be many todays.
There was a day like this one long ago
Where you swore to start loving yourself, but failed.
You stayed in bed. You overate to numb the loneliness.
You killed time however you could.
You engaged when you just wanted to cuddle.
You stopped asking yourself questions.
You put a lid on your creative edge.
You gave in to the urge to connect with those
Who had stopped deserving your time long ago.

Then you had an epiphany
While watching a movie or reading a quote.
And for a few hours, you succeeded.
Maybe even days or weeks.
It was almost like today never happened.
What could've been so bad?
You went shopping, got lost in the fragrance section,
And drove home with bags of colorful toys.

Then you came to another today.
Spiraled downward and resolved to change again.
You tried to free yourself from the self-loathing of regrets,
Places you didn't fit in, behavior you're ashamed of,
People you couldn't change,
People's perceptions of you that you couldn't improve.
People you couldn't make love you.
As if everything rested on them doing just that.

And then you got fed up of being fed up.
You read a great book.
You chatted with an enlightened friend.
You saw a counselor that gave a damn.
You went to sleep at night
And woke up while there was still daylight.
You ate nutritious things as if you deserved them,
And you exercised as if you were worth taking care of.

When out of nowhere, something triggered it. The tape.
The criticism and rejections that wounded you a decade ago.
They circled your brain. Bullied everything else out.
Soon, you are held captive again in your head.
Had you not forgotten, forgiven, or at least moved on?
You tried to get them to stop,
But just hear what your dad yelled at your mom that time.

You recall the feeling of being an outcast
At several stages, compounded like interest.
The most recent heartbreak sits on a pile of all the others.
Every time there is pain,
It brings back the memory and emotions you experienced
When you first felt this pain and all the times following it.
You are not hurting about today.
You are hurting about 30 years and today.

Time passes.
You get distracted by something beautiful.
You laugh by mistake.
Simple things make you happy like a good avocado.
God is good. Friends are everything.
You are a little less affected by every past hurt at home,
At school, at work, with friends, with men...

Then a song plays. It brings you back.
Why couldn't I make it work?
You see a picture. It draws you in.
Why wasn't I enough?
Career stress. Instead of facing this, I'd rather hide.
Back to bed. Friends call. Why did you flake? Wait—
I thought I got better.

And so, it never ends.
Healing is a process with no finish.
Giving up after a relapse into a deep blue mood
Is where many people lose
Hope, faith, and retreat in despair.
Today is always today, but there's always tomorrow.
Fighting it is overcoming. Not every time, but overall.
There can be many battles lost and still a war won.
I believe. I have to.
I believe for you too.

Muse

Some need to be blinding;
Some need to be blind.
We all demand the truth back
And still tell our lies.

We don't know where it's going,
But we know where it's not.
We are born in magenta.
Each day, toned down by life's blot.

I dreamt of being a light slideshow.
The world changing colors through me
With every different shade of gel.
Who hasn't wanted to show
What they never could tell.

I got a lifetime to kill; I'd like to kill it with you.
I used to tell my story,
But now I realize that it's ours to share.
Because nothing I'm feeling is new to be felt here.

You know you're infected
When someone turns you on
When they're not even there.
You just envision their body's frame;
It's what you wear.

Speak to me in foreign tongues.
Wear something forbidden on your neck.
I want to have to try,
But I don't want to break from the stretch.

It's not the person,
But the creativity they infuse that we actually use.
Go away now,
But return again, my muse.

A Full Life

My hemline's high.
My eye's not dry.
I left a few tears ago
And haven't been back since.

I lead a full life.

They know me at that spot.
I venture out on rides when I feel restless.
I drive aimless and end up
In sin, bed, debt, love, or danger.

I live full.

I hike. I travel to places I can't pronounce.
I learned another language.
Wrote my memoir in Spanish.

I lived out a full life.

I ordered the lobster.
Licked truffle oil off my thumb.
Sang karaoke in London because it sounded fun.

My fashion is irreverent. Deliciously don't give a damn.
Lived it up. I forgot my lover five minutes after we broke up—
Mind control.

I lived.

I went abroad, okay?
Didn't just lay on the beach. I vibed with locals.
Mixed some culture in perfume.
Came home with more lessons and insights than gifts.

I lived a full, full life.

I got a master's because well, it sounded good.

I changed careers
When I no longer felt fire,
But termites in my skin as if it were wood.

I lived, man.

I cut my hair short to that confident length
Where you can't help
But feel like an androgynous badass.

I lived such a fat, full life.

But it's a lie, babe.
A myth of epic proportion.
I was posting the hottest photo of me
With 'friends' I hardly knew,
At a spot I don't like,
While I was at home
Popping pimples,
Spray tanning ten pounds away,
Tweezing grey hairs,
Giving side eye to new wrinkles,
Ordering takeout for one that could feed three,
Hustling to maintain income,
Checking a profile compulsively,
And keeping myself company with TV.
Thinking about that trip I never took
To Greece at 23. I'm 33.

That's why half this poem is
Past tense and half presently.
The percentage that's dead in the living.

I watch people paid to act
Like people living full lives
On wide screen TV,
And I live through them.
They're not even alive.
And isn't that what we all want to say at the end?
I lived a full life?

But there's just one thing:
This universe of fear between us.

Mom

I look at my mother with fascination.
Can you really grasp someone you know so well?
Yet I see her sometimes like it's the first time.

You get so used to a person,
Their voice and presence,
That you don't know what it's like
To live removed.

I think of her longingly already,
Glimpsing the depravity I will exist in when she is gone.
I want to hold every breath hostage
Of the life we still have together.

Who am I when not in relation to her?

New Friend

The put-together you bores me.

I want to see mascara streaks coming from your eyes.

I want to see your passion felt.

I want you to open up about problems.

I don't want you to worry what I'll think.

I think you're truly masterful.

I know you're art that breathes.

Conundrum

I like some traditions, and ignore the rest.
Don't blindly support agendas, right, or left.
Passionately centrist,
Always looking for a collective best interest.

You can't count on me
To mirror a side.
You have to make sense.
And make sense with love.
Mix it with feeling.

I like many kinds of music
And identify with each decade.
I feel girly sometimes,
And other times, like a unisex musk.
Find every shade of man attractive
And don't judge women for
Being sexually conscious
Or God forbid—active.

But they want to box me in
So I'm easy to label.
They want me to be a classy, business owner.
Or a sultry bombshell.
Or a quirky artist.
Or defined by an episode of depression.
Or devout if I have religion.
Or a defender of my race by default.
Or a democrat or a republican.

Makes my head spin.
Don't know how to react
To be reacted to the way I want.
And that's the problem.
Being for the sake of being seen
A certain way.

Too many options.
We begged for this freedom.
Now it's like wearing every color of blush all at once—
A hot mess.

I speak tangential.
We're the weird ones, right?
Because we can jump all around in our heads
While still following a thread.

It's trendy to insult DJs too
Who don't spin on vinyl,
And I half feel you,
But then I think about how art innovates and evolves
While the stagnant expires.

Ever notice that
We can't block a person in real life—
Just on Facebook.
Doesn't remove them from your brain—
Just your feed.

I like to unite;
I'm a dot connecter.
Sometimes the casualty of that is connecting people
Just for them to disappear together.

The next time someone says or does
Something "wrong,"
We can remember that most just want to be
Known, loved, and understood.
When it's you,
Won't you wish they knew?

Your Purpose

Have you ever felt like
The electricity was out before inside of you?
But it all led you to this? A calling?
Like you accumulated all these connections,
Resources, and powerful, magical people around you
To release into a cause?

It's been a long time
Since I've been excited to wake up.
I woke up so late to avoid the day.
It reeked of pressure, judgment, and fear.
It felt like my inner child woke up every day
Gasping for air.

When you're doing something where your talents,
Passion, and values are aligned,
And you're appreciated for it,
You feel in your purpose.
The whole world opened up
When I joined a mission of something
Far bigger than me.

Thoughts Before Dad's Surgery

Too fragile for this life,
I float adrift and watch lessons turn into years.

Staring off into the distance,
I fold into what God has planned.
Or maybe that's called giving up
Or bad luck
Or the absolute best shot I got.

But how come as my feet graze upon the marble floor,
I've never felt so poor.
Because all I can do is hold you and pray for you,
But that alone doesn't save.
You're the subject of my adoration,
And the concept of time will take you away.

Without you, I'm bones without meat.
There's just a vast sky and land
And no direction. No reason.
No joy in sharing what becomes.
I can't manage the weight of that
Emptiness and quiet.

The anxiety purrs out of me like a cat
Overdosed on caffeine.
Then, the dulling relaxation of a vape
Buffers the edges, and I can't feel either end.

All I know is that
Memories are rehashing in waking hours.
Little glimpses of times we've had.
Times that have gradually made me
And stained me into who I am.

Fear of losing the most important people to me
Paralyzes the moment
And makes it impossible
To grab something natural from it.
It's manipulated like a subject
By the eye of its photographer.

I'm just trying to extrapolate meaning, humor—
Something legendary to make
This sweet and sour time feel
Most productive when I look back.

I want to uncover the aged glory
And what made you tick.
You can't say what if—
If I had this resource then,
I would have said, done, or gone instead.

But the now of each moment eludes me.
You are too precious to not imagine.
The idea of your absence concludes me.

A shining hour, preludes of me
Dipping into an infinite wash of grey
Where I aim to breathe and beat
Without my pulse and beacon.

Feels like a parent waving at a child
When she's dropped at school for the first time.
You're never coming back, the kid thinks,
And neither is the person I was
When you were alive.

Nights Like This

I hate nights like this.

It's just me and the music.

Me and a bottle of wine.

The fire of a forest in flames.

And a cold, dry, dark door

Between me and my wildest imagination.

Insecurity Pervades

Governed by emotion like the tides
And our bodies—mostly made of water—
By the moon,
I tread in the deepest currents.

I hope to be swallowed up, but yet to survive.
I hope to make God proud of deciding I should be alive.

I leak out
And purpose an entire ocean
With aquatic life from my will.
From a low storage of self-love.
From harboring a hologram of you in my gut.

You need to feel the depth of emptiness.
You need to not know where you're going.
How else would you know happy when it arrives?
How else would you know love when it enters?

But what will save me? I'm only strong for you.
I can make anyone better. Who makes me better?

And I know somewhere, someone else is lonely.
And they can hear me saying their words inside.

They're lonely in a crowded room.
They're forcing a smile.
They're busy making someone laugh
To take the edge off their own life.

They're settling for an easy comfort.
They're turning to delivery and TV.
They're surfing Tinder aimless.
They're scrolling feeds mindlessly.

They're taking on a role and becoming
The character people want and need them to be.

I have the adoration of many.
If only power felt as great as love.

With Child

Why wouldn't we be terrified?
We are all dumped out of a womb
Not knowing why or what to do.
Then we are encouraged to conform,
Linger in the interim sedated.

We learn that we will all die
And that everyone we love will too.
And we will have to watch and endure it.

That we will like people, and they will reject us.
We will like people, and they will like us back
And then, leave.
We will leave them too.

In the meantime,
We are supposed to find our passion,
Excel at it, and make money.
And when we get in the rhythm to survive,
We lose sight of that passion, the reason,
Our purpose, our worth, our dreams.

I am carrying a burden so deep and wide.
I'm pregnant with despair.
I didn't even realize it.
Walking around with it everywhere.

No one can see this kind of pregnancy.
But I can't sit down without tension.
Can't lie down in comfort.
Can't rest on my knees.

I am on the scale now.
The child doesn't show up
In the weight.

I don't want to leave the house, the bed.
I don't want to make the meeting.
I don't have the energy to pretend.

The guilt I feel from every lie
I've told myself,
Then projected at the world,
Which then reflected back at me...

I am a sun shining
Into other people's lives
While a forest fire burns me down inside.

What do you do when you're burning?
Eat, drink, smoke, flirt.
Read, watch, plan, post, nap, work.
Distract. Evade. Bury. Fade.

I'm pregnant and in labor.
I'm giving birth to regret, heartache, and
Pain that won't come out.
I'm asking for an epidural.
They don't seem to see the need.
It's only audible and visible to me.

And I can't breathe, but I'm smiling.
And I can't save you because I'm dying.
And I can't move because
I cannot break the pose.
The caption has to be right.
Hold my wine. Shade in my nose.

I'm in a flesh cell.
I hold the key, they tell me.
And I agree.

But it's too dark to find the lock.
Or the lock won't open.
Or when it opens,
It leads to another locked door.
Or I'm getting comfortable in the misery
I know and am cradling the floor.

Or is that just the story I tell myself
In fear of freedom.
Nothing is as scary as the thought of
Inactivated promise
Except reaching it.

Nostalgia Season

I miss (almost) everything.
Handwriting. Love letters.
Hard copy photos.
Phone calls on the land line.
Wandering outside with no sense of time.
Roller blades and the reservoir.
Endless pool days braiding string bracelets.
Innocent crushes at summer camp.
(Adults should get summers off too.)
Sleepovers without cell phones.
Watching one movie a hundred times.
Dancing to the jukebox.
Hot tubs and Friendly's ice cream.
Little Caesars and Blockbuster runs.
Oblivious to what I and the world would become.
Boredom leading to reading, writing,
Drawing, talking, and exploring.
The given support of a family unit.
Loving dogs waiting at home for you.
Holidays, special dinners, and parties,
All punctuated by music.
Having an actual group of friends.
Never facing a problem alone.
I miss the you I knew back then
And the me you knew in 1992.

Independence (Day) Life

Red for the passion
As a sweet, salted Bloody Mary stings my tongue.
White for the reflection
Of all the colors I emit at once.
Blue for the serene backdrop
Of a mindset I choose.

Free of British rule.
At our best, free of us versus them and me versus you.
Free of the delicious wounds
We identified with and held on to.

Independence is not a day; It's daily.
America is an idea in practice—
Like our human nature—
Torn between inherent goodness
And its polar opposition.

Our canvas is born clear
And then painted by love, pain, and/or fear
That accumulates like dust over time.
We will always fight for freedom
From the vices that reside within our minds.

But this can be a joyous fight.
Works in progress can fail at many tries
And still meet an overall outcome of right.
I aim and miss, but aim again
To embody the spirit today and for life.

ABOUT THE AUTHOR

Heidi L. Klotzman is an award-winning CEO and personality based in Baltimore, Maryland. In 2005, she founded HeidnSeek Entertainment (hnseek.com), a company recognized for its excellence in marketing businesses and events and booking live music and DJ talent.

Raised in a musical household, Klotzman found a first love in music, but her second love was writing. Her mom would read to her frequently, and she learned to express her thoughts, feelings, and creativity through poetry. She accumulated hundreds of poems over the years. Her biggest writing influences were song lyrics from various genres, hip-hop, and poets: Carl Hancock Rux and Paul Beatty.

She has performed her poetry at her alma maters, Roland Park Country School (RPCS), Eugene Lang Writing Seminar College, and Goucher College, as well as at special events in Baltimore and New York. When she graduated RPCS, she was named *The Poetic Soul of the School* by the then head of school.

Klotzman thanks God, her parents, grandparents, teachers, classmates, editors, and friends for encouraging her to express herself in writing. This book is her journey across love, loss, growth, and acceptance through poetry. She hopes that she can reach someone else the way that other poets have reached her.